G.R.A.S.P. Prayer Journal
A 10-week journey toward transforming your devotion with God

Rachael Allina

UNITED ≫→ HOUSE

G.R.A.S.P. Prayer Journal—Copyright ©2024 by Rachael Allina

Published by UNITED HOUSE Publishing
All rights reserved. No portion of this book may be reproduced or shared in any form—electronic, printed, photocopied, recording, or by any information storage and retrieval system, without prior written permission from the publisher. The use of short quotations is permitted.

ISBN: 978-1-952840-53-1

UNITED HOUSE Publishing
Waterford, Michigan
info@unitedhousepublishing.com
www.unitedhousepublishing.com

Cover Layout and Interior Design:
Rachael Allina and United House Publishing

Printed in the United States of America
2024—First Edition

SPECIAL SALES
Most UNITED HOUSE books are available at special quantity discounts when purchased in bulk by corporations, organizations, and special-interest groups. For information, please e-mail orders@unitedhousepublishing.com

This journal belongs to :

_____

Hello beloved!
God delights in you, you are His daughter! He loves you and desires to draw you closer in your relationship with Him.

Have you ever felt unsure of what to pray or how to pray, or are you stagnant in your prayer life? Or maybe you want to enhance your prayer life with more intention and depth. Wherever you are, this journal is designed to help you increase your prayer life with consistency.

The G.R.A.S.P. Prayer method was inspired by my personal prayer process, which He revealed to me as I journaled.

The G.R.A.S.P. acronym stands for:

G - Gratitude
R - Repent
A - Armor
S - Surrender
P - Petition

Not only did I love the intention behind each word in the acronym, but also the definition. The definition of grasp is "to hold firmly," and I believe that prayer is one of the most powerful ways we can stay close to Him. I was initially inspired to make stack bracelets of each G.R.A.S.P word for accountability to encourage communication with Him throughout the day. Since then, I have felt a desire for an even deeper devotion through journaling.

In this journal, each page has a blank journaling section under each word of the G.R.A.S.P. acronym with a prompt to help you get started journaling. It is a total of 70 days (10 weeks), which research shows is the average time it takes to make a habit.

The goal of this journal is to help you establish a habit of prayer.

One of my favorite pastors once said, "Prayer is about more than getting something. It's about being with someone—it is not a manipulation tool; it's a relational nearness."

If prayer is how we converse with God, it is worth devoting ourselves to and requires our obedience. Let us grasp Him as we take this prayer journey to the next level!

God, help us make prayer a rhythm in our lives that draws us into Your presence and peace daily so that we may walk out Your plan and purpose.

In Jesus' name, Amen!

-Rachael Allina

G.R.A.S.P.
Prayer Method

G Gratitude
Recognizing the good, that it all comes from God, and professing it in all circumstances.

R Repent
A change of mindset, heart, and action of turning from sin/self and moving in a new direction towards God.

A Armor
Swapping out old rags for righteous robes that are clothing you in Christ himself! His armor protects against spiritual assaults.

S Surrender
Saying no to self and bowing your heart to God's plan. Letting go of your will in exchange for His perfect will.

P Petition
Approaching the Lord to humbly ask Him for something you need or to intercede for another.

Today's Date: ___/___/___

GRATITUDE
Thank you for...

REPENT
Forgive me for...

ARMOR
Protect me from...

SURRENDER
Help me trust you with...

PETITION
I ask that you will...

Today's Date: ___/___/____

GRATITUDE
Thank you for...

REPENT
Forgive me for...

ARMOR
Protect me from...

SURRENDER
Help me trust you with...

PETITION
I ask that you will...

Today's Date: ___/___/___

GRATITUDE
Thank you for...

REPENT
Forgive me for...

ARMOR
Protect me from...

SURRENDER
Help me trust you with...

PETITION
I ask that you will...

Today's Date: ___/___/___

GRATITUDE
Thank you for...

REPENT
Forgive me for...

ARMOR
Protect me from...

SURRENDER
Help me trust you with...

PETITION
I ask that you will...

Today's Date: ___/___/____

GRATITUDE
Thank you for...

REPENT
Forgive me for...

ARMOR
Protect me from...

SURRENDER
Help me trust you with...

PETITION
I ask that you will...

Today's Date: ___/___/___

GRATITUDE
Thank you for...

REPENT
Forgive me for...

ARMOR
Protect me from...

SURRENDER
Help me trust you with...

PETITION
I ask that you will...

Today's Date: ___/___/____

GRATITUDE
Thank you for...

REPENT
Forgive me for...

ARMOR
Protect me from...

SURRENDER
Help me trust you with...

PETITION
I ask that you will...

Today's Date: ___/___/___

GRATITUDE
Thank you for...

REPENT
Forgive me for...

ARMOR
Protect me from...

SURRENDER
Help me trust you with...

PETITION
I ask that you will...

Today's Date: ___/___/___

GRATITUDE
Thank you for...

REPENT
Forgive me for...

ARMOR
Protect me from...

SURRENDER
Help me trust you with...

PETITION
I ask that you will...

Today's Date: ___/___/___

GRATITUDE
Thank you for...

REPENT
Forgive me for...

ARMOR
Protect me from...

SURRENDER
Help me trust you with...

PETITION
I ask that you will...

Today's Date: ___/___/___

GRATITUDE
Thank you for...

REPENT
Forgive me for...

ARMOR
Protect me from...

SURRENDER
Help me trust you with...

PETITION
I ask that you will...

Today's Date: ___/___/____

GRATITUDE
Thank you for...

REPENT
Forgive me for...

ARMOR
Protect me from...

SURRENDER
Help me trust you with...

PETITION
I ask that you will...

Today's Date: ___/___/___

GRATITUDE
Thank you for...

REPENT
Forgive me for...

ARMOR
Protect me from...

SURRENDER
Help me trust you with...

PETITION
I ask that you will...

Today's Date: ___/___/____

GRATITUDE
Thank you for...

REPENT
Forgive me for...

ARMOR
Protect me from...

SURRENDER
Help me trust you with...

PETITION
I ask that you will...

Today's Date: ___/___/____

GRATITUDE
Thank you for…

REPENT
Forgive me for…

ARMOR
Protect me from…

SURRENDER
Help me trust you with…

PETITION
I ask that you will…

Today's Date: ___/___/___

GRATITUDE
Thank you for...

REPENT
Forgive me for...

ARMOR
Protect me from...

SURRENDER
Help me trust you with...

PETITION
I ask that you will...

Today's Date: ___/___/____

GRATITUDE
Thank you for...

REPENT
Forgive me for...

ARMOR
Protect me from...

SURRENDER
Help me trust you with...

PETITION
I ask that you will...

Today's Date: ___/___/___

GRATITUDE
Thank you for...

REPENT
Forgive me for...

ARMOR
Protect me from...

SURRENDER
Help me trust you with...

PETITION
I ask that you will...

Today's Date: ___/___/____

GRATITUDE
Thank you for...

REPENT
Forgive me for...

ARMOR
Protect me from...

SURRENDER
Help me trust you with...

PETITION
I ask that you will...

Today's Date: ___/___/____

GRATITUDE
Thank you for...

REPENT
Forgive me for...

ARMOR
Protect me from...

SURRENDER
Help me trust you with...

PETITION
I ask that you will...

Today's Date: ___/___/____

GRATITUDE
Thank you for...

REPENT
Forgive me for...

ARMOR
Protect me from...

SURRENDER
Help me trust you with...

PETITION
I ask that you will...

Today's Date: ___/___/___

GRATITUDE
Thank you for...

REPENT
Forgive me for...

ARMOR
Protect me from...

SURRENDER
Help me trust you with...

PETITION
I ask that you will...

Today's Date: ___/___/___

GRATITUDE
Thank you for...

REPENT
Forgive me for...

ARMOR
Protect me from...

SURRENDER
Help me trust you with...

PETITION
I ask that you will...

Today's Date: ___/___/____

GRATITUDE
Thank you for...

REPENT
Forgive me for...

ARMOR
Protect me from...

SURRENDER
Help me trust you with...

PETITION
I ask that you will...

Today's Date: ___/___/____

GRATITUDE
Thank you for...

REPENT
Forgive me for...

ARMOR
Protect me from...

SURRENDER
Help me trust you with...

PETITION
I ask that you will...

Today's Date: ___/___/____

GRATITUDE
Thank you for...

REPENT
Forgive me for...

ARMOR
Protect me from...

SURRENDER
Help me trust you with...

PETITION
I ask that you will...

Today's Date: ___/___/___

GRATITUDE
Thank you for...

REPENT
Forgive me for...

ARMOR
Protect me from...

SURRENDER
Help me trust you with...

PETITION
I ask that you will...

Today's Date: ___/___/____

GRATITUDE
Thank you for...

REPENT
Forgive me for...

ARMOR
Protect me from...

SURRENDER
Help me trust you with...

PETITION
I ask that you will...

Today's Date: ___/___/____

GRATITUDE
Thank you for...

REPENT
Forgive me for...

ARMOR
Protect me from...

SURRENDER
Help me trust you with...

PETITION
I ask that you will...

Today's Date: ___/___/____

GRATITUDE
Thank you for...

REPENT
Forgive me for...

ARMOR
Protect me from...

SURRENDER
Help me trust you with...

PETITION
I ask that you will...

Today's Date: ___/___/____

GRATITUDE
Thank you for...

REPENT
Forgive me for...

ARMOR
Protect me from...

SURRENDER
Help me trust you with...

PETITION
I ask that you will...

Today's Date: ___/___/___

GRATITUDE
Thank you for...

REPENT
Forgive me for...

ARMOR
Protect me from...

SURRENDER
Help me trust you with...

PETITION
I ask that you will...

Today's Date: ___/___/___

GRATITUDE
Thank you for...

REPENT
Forgive me for...

ARMOR
Protect me from...

SURRENDER
Help me trust you with...

PETITION
I ask that you will...

Today's Date: ___/___/___

GRATITUDE
Thank you for...

REPENT
Forgive me for...

ARMOR
Protect me from...

SURRENDER
Help me trust you with...

PETITION
I ask that you will...

Today's Date: ___/___/___

GRATITUDE
Thank you for...

REPENT
Forgive me for...

ARMOR
Protect me from...

SURRENDER
Help me trust you with...

PETITION
I ask that you will...

Today's Date: ___/___/____

GRATITUDE
Thank you for...

REPENT
Forgive me for...

ARMOR
Protect me from...

SURRENDER
Help me trust you with...

PETITION
I ask that you will...

Today's Date: ___/___/___

GRATITUDE
Thank you for...

REPENT
Forgive me for...

ARMOR
Protect me from...

SURRENDER
Help me trust you with...

PETITION
I ask that you will...

Today's Date: ___/___/___

GRATITUDE
Thank you for...

REPENT
Forgive me for...

ARMOR
Protect me from...

SURRENDER
Help me trust you with...

PETITION
I ask that you will...

Today's Date: ___/___/___

GRATITUDE
Thank you for...

REPENT
Forgive me for...

ARMOR
Protect me from...

SURRENDER
Help me trust you with...

PETITION
I ask that you will...

Today's Date: ___/___/____

GRATITUDE
Thank you for...

REPENT
Forgive me for...

ARMOR
Protect me from...

SURRENDER
Help me trust you with...

PETITION
I ask that you will...

Today's Date: ___/___/___

GRATITUDE
Thank you for...

REPENT
Forgive me for...

ARMOR
Protect me from...

SURRENDER
Help me trust you with...

PETITION
I ask that you will...

Today's Date: ___/___/___

GRATITUDE
Thank you for...

REPENT
Forgive me for...

ARMOR
Protect me from...

SURRENDER
Help me trust you with...

PETITION
I ask that you will...

Today's Date: ___/___/___

GRATITUDE
Thank you for...

REPENT
Forgive me for...

ARMOR
Protect me from...

SURRENDER
Help me trust you with...

PETITION
I ask that you will...

Today's Date: ___/___/___

GRATITUDE
Thank you for...

REPENT
Forgive me for...

ARMOR
Protect me from...

SURRENDER
Help me trust you with...

PETITION
I ask that you will...

Today's Date: ___/___/____

GRATITUDE
Thank you for...

REPENT
Forgive me for...

ARMOR
Protect me from...

SURRENDER
Help me trust you with...

PETITION
I ask that you will...

Today's Date: ___/___/____

GRATITUDE
Thank you for...

REPENT
Forgive me for...

ARMOR
Protect me from...

SURRENDER
Help me trust you with...

PETITION
I ask that you will...

Today's Date: ___/___/____

GRATITUDE
Thank you for...

REPENT
Forgive me for...

ARMOR
Protect me from...

SURRENDER
Help me trust you with...

PETITION
I ask that you will...

Today's Date: ___/___/____

GRATITUDE
Thank you for...

REPENT
Forgive me for...

ARMOR
Protect me from...

SURRENDER
Help me trust you with...

PETITION
I ask that you will...

Today's Date: ___/___/___

GRATITUDE
Thank you for...

REPENT
Forgive me for...

ARMOR
Protect me from...

SURRENDER
Help me trust you with...

PETITION
I ask that you will...

Today's Date: ___/___/___

GRATITUDE
Thank you for...

REPENT
Forgive me for...

ARMOR
Protect me from...

SURRENDER
Help me trust you with...

PETITION
I ask that you will...

Today's Date: ___/___/____

GRATITUDE
Thank you for...

REPENT
Forgive me for...

ARMOR
Protect me from...

SURRENDER
Help me trust you with...

PETITION
I ask that you will...

Today's Date: ___/___/___

GRATITUDE
Thank you for...

REPENT
Forgive me for...

ARMOR
Protect me from...

SURRENDER
Help me trust you with...

PETITION
I ask that you will...

Today's Date: ___/___/____

GRATITUDE
Thank you for...

REPENT
Forgive me for...

ARMOR
Protect me from...

SURRENDER
Help me trust you with...

PETITION
I ask that you will...

Today's Date: ___/___/____

GRATITUDE
Thank you for...

REPENT
Forgive me for...

ARMOR
Protect me from...

SURRENDER
Help me trust you with...

PETITION
I ask that you will...

Today's Date: ___/___/____

GRATITUDE
Thank you for...

REPENT
Forgive me for...

ARMOR
Protect me from...

SURRENDER
Help me trust you with...

PETITION
I ask that you will...

Today's Date: ___/___/____

GRATITUDE
Thank you for...

REPENT
Forgive me for...

ARMOR
Protect me from...

SURRENDER
Help me trust you with...

PETITION
I ask that you will...

Today's Date: ___/___/____

GRATITUDE
Thank you for...

REPENT
Forgive me for...

ARMOR
Protect me from...

SURRENDER
Help me trust you with...

PETITION
I ask that you will...

Today's Date: ___/___/___

GRATITUDE
Thank you for...

REPENT
Forgive me for...

ARMOR
Protect me from...

SURRENDER
Help me trust you with...

PETITION
I ask that you will...

Today's Date: ___/___/____

GRATITUDE
Thank you for...

REPENT
Forgive me for...

ARMOR
Protect me from...

SURRENDER
Help me trust you with...

PETITION
I ask that you will...

Today's Date: ___/___/____

GRATITUDE
Thank you for…

REPENT
Forgive me for…

ARMOR
Protect me from…

SURRENDER
Help me trust you with…

PETITION
I ask that you will…

Today's Date: ___/___/____

GRATITUDE
Thank you for...

REPENT
Forgive me for...

ARMOR
Protect me from...

SURRENDER
Help me trust you with...

PETITION
I ask that you will...

Today's Date: ___/___/____

GRATITUDE
Thank you for...

REPENT
Forgive me for...

ARMOR
Protect me from...

SURRENDER
Help me trust you with...

PETITION
I ask that you will...

Today's Date: ___/___/____

GRATITUDE
Thank you for...

REPENT
Forgive me for...

ARMOR
Protect me from...

SURRENDER
Help me trust you with...

PETITION
I ask that you will...

Today's Date: ___/___/___

GRATITUDE
Thank you for...

REPENT
Forgive me for...

ARMOR
Protect me from...

SURRENDER
Help me trust you with...

PETITION
I ask that you will...

Today's Date: ___/___/___

GRATITUDE
Thank you for...

REPENT
Forgive me for...

ARMOR
Protect me from...

SURRENDER
Help me trust you with...

PETITION
I ask that you will...

Today's Date: ___/___/____

GRATITUDE
Thank you for...

REPENT
Forgive me for...

ARMOR
Protect me from...

SURRENDER
Help me trust you with...

PETITION
I ask that you will...

Today's Date: ___/___/____

GRATITUDE
Thank you for...

REPENT
Forgive me for...

ARMOR
Protect me from...

SURRENDER
Help me trust you with...

PETITION
I ask that you will...

Today's Date: ___/___/___

GRATITUDE
Thank you for...

REPENT
Forgive me for...

ARMOR
Protect me from...

SURRENDER
Help me trust you with...

PETITION
I ask that you will...

Today's Date: ___/___/___

GRATITUDE
Thank you for...

REPENT
Forgive me for...

ARMOR
Protect me from...

SURRENDER
Help me trust you with...

PETITION
I ask that you will...

Today's Date: ___/___/___

GRATITUDE
Thank you for...

REPENT
Forgive me for...

ARMOR
Protect me from...

SURRENDER
Help me trust you with...

PETITION
I ask that you will...

About the Author

Rachael Allina and her husband, Adam, live in Asheville, NC, where they are raising three young children. They are embracing a homeschool and homesteading lifestyle, which contrasts significantly with their upbringing in Chicago, IL. They are active members of their church, where they are dedicated to building and nurturing their community.

Rachael's journey in the beauty industry led her to become an entrepreneur in 2015. She is a professional makeup artist, author, and philanthropist. Her passion for beauty and fashion and her mission to spread the gospel inspired her to launch the Broken Made Beauty boutique. Collaborations with vendors support various trauma survivors and contribute to the Broken Made Beautiful nonprofit organization she founded in 2021. This organization's mission is to provide Christ-centered resources for survivors of sexual trauma.

You can always find her with a cup of coffee in hand and wearing the G.R.A.S.P. prayer bracelets on her wrists!

www.ingramcontent.com/pod-product-compliance
Lightning Source LLC
Chambersburg PA
CBHW061810070526
44586CB00024B/2794